Fire And Moonlight (also on cover page) ~ *This image was inspired by a camping adventure. The glimmering full moon, casting a luminous glow over the lake. A crackling fire on a cool summer evening. A crisp gentle breeze keeps the bugs down. Releasing all the stress of life, allowing things to be put into a much simpler perspective.*

Dedication

This book is dedicated to all the family, friends, galleries, and all the people who have purchased my art, or offered praise and encouragement for my efforts over the last ten years. Thank you all for your support, allowing me to follow my dreams. Hopefully the next ten years will be even greater than the last.

Designed and published in 2004 by **Jackpine Design Studio Ltd.**, Grande Prairie, Alberta, Canada.

Printed in Alberta, Canada by Quebecor World through Jackpine Design, Grande Prairie, Alberta, Canada.

Table Of Contents

Introduction

Growing up in the wilds of Northern British Columbia, you can't help but be influenced by its rugged, breathtaking beauty & vast numbers of wildlife. Fort Nelson is a remote area with endless spaces to explore in all directions. Now that I've travelled around a little, I've come to realize what an amazing & unique experience I was privileged to be in, basically my backyard was as big as your eye could see.

I have always been a huge admirer of wildlife and aboriginal art from back to my childhood. I have tried to create my own style in a medium not widely popular with mainstream art circles, being pencil, but it seems to be building. My work is far from traditional pencil drawing from a technical point of view, but I feel it is part of its appeal and originality.

Over the last ten years I have produced over 170 limited edition pencil prints depicting wildlife and aboriginal-influenced works. This book is a collection of some of the images I have done over my career. Ten years as a struggling artist is an amazing milestone for a guy with no real training and exposure, or financial backing. I guess it's called paying my dues. I hope the people buying this book enjoy the work, and I leave much open to their interpretation of anything they can get out of it. The work is far from traditional but I hope it pays homage to our great wilderness, nature, and aboriginal cultures.

The Early Years

Wolf "Tracker" ~ *This is one of the earliest prints I have done. I have always had a great fascination with wolves. The first time I saw a wolf I was ten. We were camped up by Tetsa River with my family. I was walking along a small path beside a little creek when I saw a black wolf. He was at the edge of the tree line. We looked at each other with a casual glance and he went off into the bush and I went on to the cabin. I've never forgotten that.*

Tiger ~ *This head portrait was inspired by the absolute respect these big cats demand. I really think this is one of the most majestic and striking animals in the world. Hopefully it can be saved from extinction.*

9

Elders Spirit ~ *This image is a tribute to the wisdom and strength of a once great people, rich in culture and spirit.*

10

These three pieces just express some of the diverse images along the west coast of Canada, from north to south.

Cabin And Canoe

Bears Fishin'

Killer Whales

Cougar On The Beach ~ *A softer more safe look at a graceful "power house" taking a stroll along a Vancouver Island beach. During my time on Vancouver Island, I was fortunate not to run into one of these powerful and swift predators, but I did see a lot of tracks...*

Morning After Abstract Face ~ *This abstract design was a throw-back to a reckless youth of wild partying. The image reflects what a teenaged hangover looks like in the mirror.*

Bald Eagle With Fish ~ *This design depicts a Bald Eagle about to enjoy the fruits of its labours. Who wouldn't like a tasty fish fresh out of the water...*

Raven "Last Tree" ~ *This non-traditional Haida stylized Raven is a symbol of ever-diminishing national resources. A Raven perched on the last tree with a tear on its face.*

Wolf Pack And Raven ~ *This image expresses the relationship of wolves, ravens, and moose in nature.*

15

Wolf ~ *A simple portrait of a playful wolf looking around a tree investigating his surroundings. His breaths mists in the cool winter air while the Northern Lights dance in the background.*

16

Wolf And Track ~ *A portrait of wolves in a series of states stretched on a hide frame.*

Wolf ~ *The spirit of the wolf embodied in man.*

Horses ~
This image embodies the horses' use with aboriginal people of the past.

20

Horse - "Seed Demon"

This is my attempt at humor. A horse named Seed Demon ready for action... Advertising pays.

21

Lone Wolf ~ *A solitary wolf head portrait with a gentle smile. The silhouette of a howling wolf asking the Northern Lights to dance to its serenade.*

Rivals - Grizzly & Eagle (facing page) ~ *This print shows the relationship of these great natural fishermen co-existing in the wild. Man should be this evolved…*

CALVIN D CORNISH 2002

Wolves & Ravens ~ *Joined in song, soothing the pack with a gentle lullaby as they settle in for the evening.*

Coyote - Night Howl (facing page) ~ *The haunting cry of the coyote. Silhouetted by a full moon, the beautiful shape of a coyote frames an image of a bugling elk. To bring my own flair to this rugged northern image, I surrounded the picture with a distinct southwest abstract design to show its wide range of habitat to the south as well. The oval shape accentuates the howling coyote and draws the eye inward to the mature bull elk.*

"NIGHT HOWL" COYOTE.
CALVIN CORNISH. 2002 ©

Wolves ~ *A family of wolves howling in the moonlight. In the foreground two Magpies straggle along for the ride, scavenging for leftovers of a winter kill. The inset shows a different vision of a howling wolf. Maybe an answer from another pack...*

Grey Ghost Wolf ~ *A solitary wolf out for an evening stroll in the moonlight. Its spiritual image design enlarged in the full moon.*

Grizzly ~ *A portrait of a Grizzly Bear with an aboriginal influenced design of a bear taking a bath in a river, basking in the sunlight.*

27

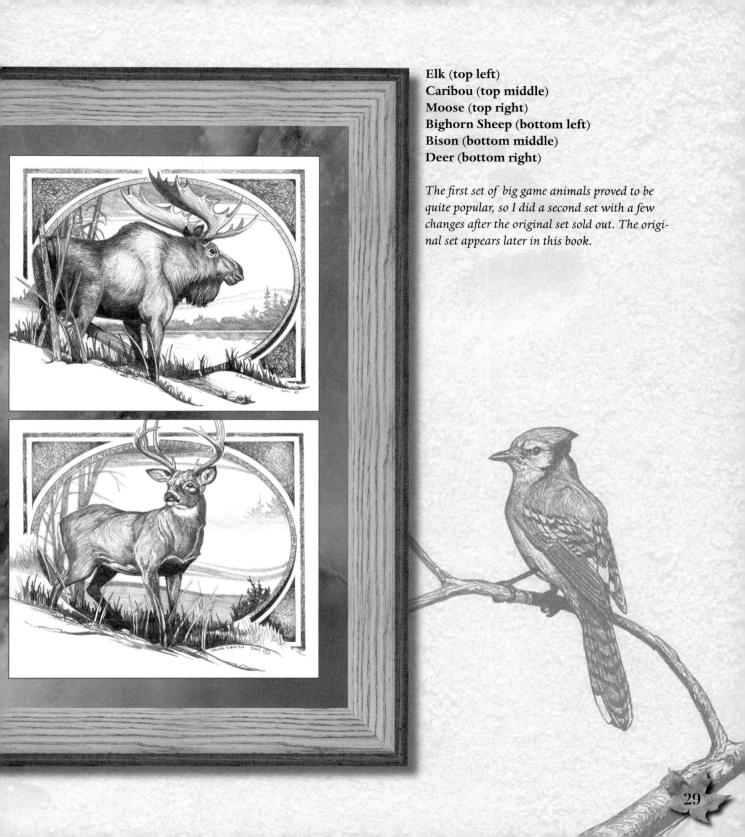

Elk **(top left)**
Caribou **(top middle)**
Moose **(top right)**
Bighorn Sheep **(bottom left)**
Bison **(bottom middle)**
Deer **(bottom right)**

The first set of big game animals proved to be quite popular, so I did a second set with a few changes after the original set sold out. The original set appears later in this book.

29

Sea Otter ~ *This is one of the most fascinating seashore creatures I know. Its mannerisms and use of its hands almost give it a human-like characteristic. These incredible animals were hunted to near extinction for their soft, thick, lustrous fur. The world's sea otter population has rebounded somewhat due to great conservation efforts. Recent transplants have re-established Sea Otters along parts of the British Columbia coast where it had been completely wiped out, allowing for rare, but ever increasing sightings that are a real treat.*

Polar Bear ~ *An absolute king of the arctic. Unfortunately, an ever-increasingly rare site. The Inukshuk, another arctic symbol, shows man's intrusion on the bears' habitat.*

Seal Pup ~ *One look into the cute baby face of a pup Harp Seal could melt the toughest heart. At birth, the pups are covered with a long, fluffy white fur from which they are affectionately called "Whitecoats."*

The pups nurse for only about 2 weeks before they are abandoned to fend for themselves. During that two week period they grow enormously. When they are weaned, they weigh 40-45 kg. Despite the sealers, sharks, killer whales and polar bears, these beautiful creatures apparently live for up to 30 years or more.

Cougar "Out of the Shadows

My time on Vancouver Island inspired this image. A very reclusive but predatory animal, the cougar is an amazing sight to see - but maybe not from this close...

Cougar "Out of the Shadows"

31

Bison - "Silenced Thunder" ~ *A tribute to a noble animal that was almost completely wiped off our planet. This image shows the grandeur of this magnificent creature and the one thing that could take its earth-shaking herds to the rare sight they have become.*

32

Black Bear And Raven ~ *A Black Bear saunters along a lake's edge while a few ravens tag along in hopes of a free meal.*

Grizzly! ~ *I've never personally been in this situation. This image was inspired as a play on who's boss at the local fishin' hole...*

Wolves - "Spring Thaw" (facing page) ~ *A close family gathering. Lighthearted moment after a long winter, spring is finally upon them. A hint of melting snow and a Blue Jay close by signifying renewal and growth.*

Canadian Lynx ~ *Several years back while driving to Fort Nelson in winter I came across a Lynx crossing the highway. I had to pull over to watch it. Usually they just run off into the bushes before you can really get a good look. This one, however, stood in a little clearing beside the road staring back at me from about 40 feet away. "Just my luck... I forgot my camera." This image is a loose interpretation of that day.*

Wolves "Spring thaw"   159/200

Black Bear ~ *Don't let this cuddly, inviting face fool you. Black Bears are truly one of the most misunderstood and unpredicatable of all Canadian omnivores. These bears are often seen foraging for berries and tender grasses through the spring and summer months, but are just as likely to partake of a good carnivorous meal as anything else. Sadly, I've seen too many incidences of its entanglement with man, with tragic results.*

Foxes And Hare - "Lucky" ~ *'Nuff said!*

37

Wild Horse ~ *A tribute to an uncomplicated way of life; cowboys and wild herds of horses. If you look close, this paint has riders camouflaged in the design pattern on its body.*

Within the artwork: *Calvin Cornish .96 ©*

Wolves ~ *This portrait shows a gentle and more natural side to the wolf than depicted in traditional folklore. Also, this*

image shows other animals roles in nature in relationship to the wolf.

Fireside Gathering

A "Dr. Doolittle" type of communicating with nature, but not likely something you would ever see in reality.

Wolf Track (facing page) ~ *An image inspired by Bev Doolittle's genius in combining images. This one is a light-hearted look at what wolves dream about.*

43

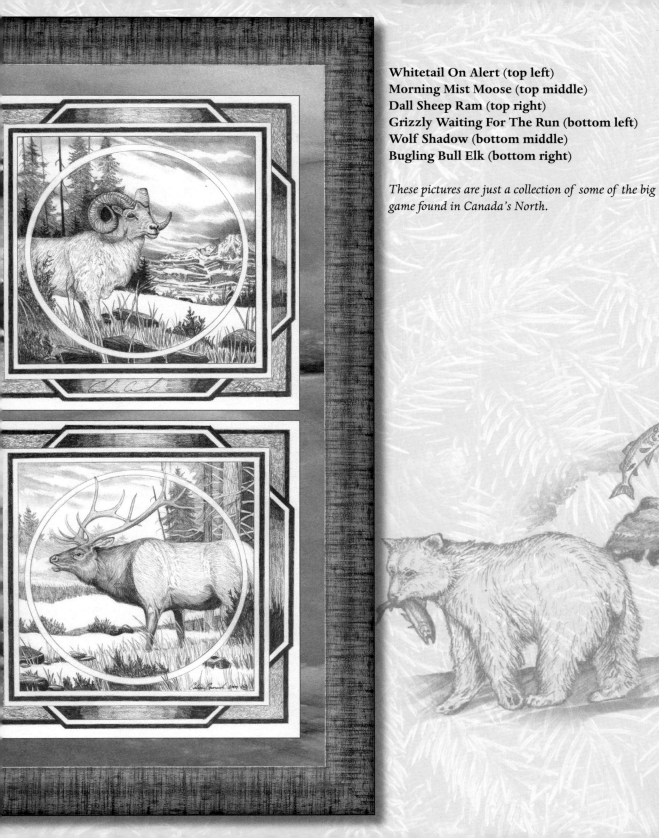

Whitetail On Alert (top left)
Morning Mist Moose (top middle)
Dall Sheep Ram (top right)
Grizzly Waiting For The Run (bottom left)
Wolf Shadow (bottom middle)
Bugling Bull Elk (bottom right)

These pictures are just a collection of some of the big game found in Canada's North.

Thunder And Lightning ~ *Bighorns at battle, the ear-shattering crack of their horns as they square off for supremacy.*

46

"THUNDER & LIGHTNING"

Mustang Heart ~ *In this image, I tried to express the spirit of a herd of wild mustangs thundering across a rolling plain with mountains and figurative wind-swept clouds complimenting the scene.*

Birds Of A Feather

49

Kingfisher ~ *From one king fisher to another... A beautiful northern setting with rolling mountains, deep forests, and fast-paced waterfalls; a place where Ospreys and Kingfishers co-exist.*

Golden Eagle (facing page) ~ *A portrait of a bird of beauty and grace with a golden brown hue and a deadly grip. A magnificent predator.*

Calvin Cornish / 2000 ©

Eagle - "Spotted Prey" ~ *A majestic Bald Eagle lifts off of an old snag as it spots a ready meal.*

Eagle Pride ~ *The soaring freedom of an uplifted figure with a touch of Canadian pride.*

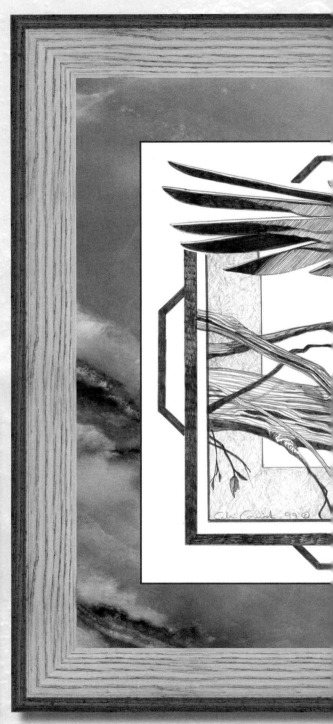

53

Loons ~ *Common Loons are fascinating to watch. A stunning and handsome bird with an absolutely haunting cry with magnificent, contrasting black and white plumage.*

Arctic Loon ~ *This striking pose from an amazing aquatic bird. Arctic Loons are one of the most acrobatic water birds found in Canada. One of their most commonly seen poses is raising their bodies out of the water to signal alertness or create a distraction. The Arctic Loon breeds on the tundra, and is usually found only on the west coast in winter. It rarely wanders as far eastward as the Peace Region, but has occasionally been seen and heard in the early parts of winter before the ice takes over.*

Tundra Swan ~ *A graceful white bird swimming along the edge of a lake, the background washed out in a light mist of fog.*

Bald Eagle ~ *The dramatic angle of this image helps create a feeling of reverence or majesty about this strong and capable bird. The wind ruffling its feathers shows its strength and ability to survive in a harsh climate. A flying eagle in the border gives the impression of exactly how large and strong this raptor really is.*

Great Blue Heron ~ *This stylized design is of one of the most stunning fishermen to inhabit the northern lakeshores.*

Canada Geese ~ *A great Canadian symbol and an amazing bird in flight. Their strong distinctive call is associated with the advent of spring and fall. These birds mate for life, and the family group remains together for several months after the young hatch. This image represents that solid bond. Through all things, these great Canadian icons remain together, as the stormy background indicates.*

Great Horned Owl ~ *This magnificent bird's complicated plumage provides great camouflage amongst the branches of a nesting area; the piercing stare of its large bright eyes gives away its position.*

Eagle And Harley ~ *Cruising down an open road, soaring high in the open sky. Two symbolic images of freedom and open spaces.*

Golden Eagle ~ *A proud and noble bird of prey, the Golden Eagle is one of the most respectable Canadian creatures I know. This portrait study is my way of trying to show the magnitude and presence of this true hunter.*

62

Bald Eagle
This portrait, inlayed with a West Coast Haida eagle design, embodies the Bald Eagle's spirit.

63

Osprey - "A Time To Dream" ~ *The spirit of the fisherman at one with nature. The Osprey; one of nature's best fishermen. Kindred spirits.*

Eagle Fisherman (facing page) ~ *This image expresses the love people have for fishing and its relevance to one of nature's greatest fishermen. The silhouette is a re-creation of a trip friends and I went on back in our high school days.*

CALVIN CORNISH/2001

Blue Heron ~ *A stylized portrait of a magnificent fisher, at the ready on a river's edge.*

Eagle ~ *A portrait design of a majestic bird of prey, mixed with some aboriginal influence.*

67

Three Song Birds ~ *In a variety of typical Canadian landscape settings*

Calvin Cornish 97©

Eagle "Let Freedom Reign" ~ *This image was inspired after the events of 9.11. It is a tribute to our way of life as North Americans. Freedom of spirit is and always will be unbreakable.*

American Kestrel ~ *A colourful rustic orange and blue bird, this small hawk has a much less threatening look than his bigger cousins.*

Within the artwork: CALVIN D CORNISH / 2003 ©

Eagle ~ *This print was a homage to a majestic bird of prey. It was my own take on a West Coast aboriginal design.*

Golden Eagle Kayak ~ *Kayaking is a very relaxing and spirit-lifting endeavor. The eagle represents the freedom and serenity of flight you can get while gliding over a smooth lake in an open space with nothing but the sounds of nature to surround you.*

Eagle (left) ~ *A proud head portrait wrapped by an aboriginal-influenced design. Part of my study in pen & ink.*

Loons (right)~ *A pair of Arctic Loons; their elegant plumage dancing in an aboriginal-inspired reflection.*

Swan - "Tribute To A Trumpeter"

This image was a tribute to the generous spirit of the people of Grande Prairie, the "Swan City". Profits from the sale of this image are going to the Food Bank to help people make ends meet. Coming from a humble background, I know just how difficult it can be. This print is available through the Salvation Army thrift store in Grande Prairie.

75

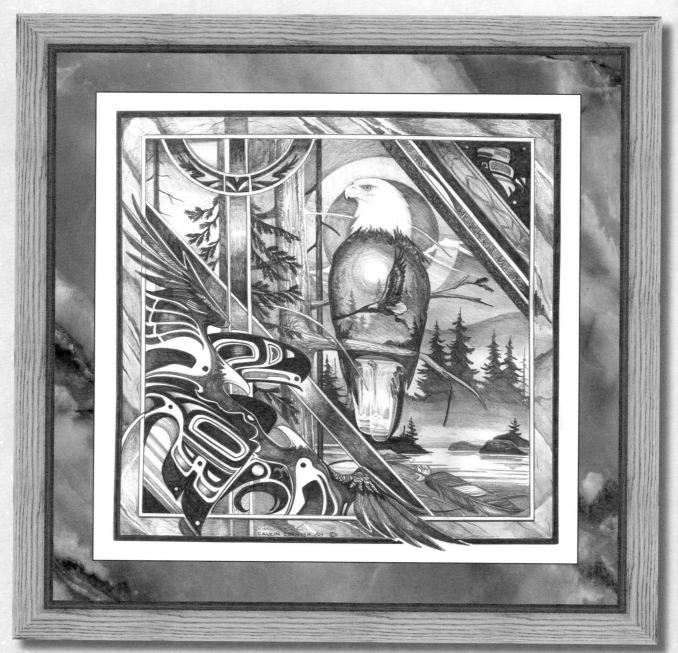

Eagle's Domain ~ *Eagles have always facinated me. This image is a mixture of eagles (pictures in pictures) paying homage to a North American king of the sky.*

Sunset Campsite

This image was a recollection of a campsite in the Yukon. The still waters beckoning the sun to set upon the horizon, a warm fire waiting to heat a chilled soul as the temperature drops with the sun. One of the greatest places and moments in life.

Northern Lights & Dog Sled

This image, as well as "Gold Panner" and "Sunset Campsite", was inspired by the time I have spent in the Yukon. It is truly an incredible and unique place to be. It is worth visiting at least once in your life.

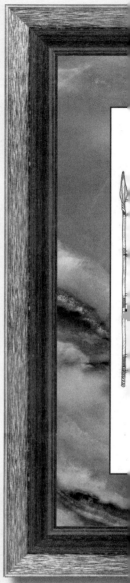

Gold Panner (facing page) ~ *I have spent a fair bit of time in the Yukon. It is a very different and unique way of life compared to even most other parts of Canada. The panner and his husky relaxing by a river edge. Panners were from a breed of men only found in the rugged corners of the world. They spend their lives toiling through the silt and stones, hoping to find a little piece of history.*

Ghost Warrior ~ *This image was a tribute to an amazing culture and spirit of the past. Part of the goal of this particular piece was to encourage pride in one's heritage and help aboriginals to maintain their place in a modern world.*

81

Summer Breeze ~ *A beautiful woman, hair flowing gently from a warm summer breeze. A vision that could stop almost any man in his tracks...*

Huntress (**facing page**) ~ *A woman in a bear clan prepared for a hunt. Her gazing stare focused on the task at hand.*

Nanaimo Harbour Bench ~ *When I moved away from the island, on my way to the ferry, I stopped to take one last look along the harbour. The sun was just coming up, and the view was amazing. I took a picture of the harbour. It really is a lasting impression and I hope to visit the west coast again soon.*

Rockface Waterfall ~ *This waterfall actually exists, but I think I'm the only one who was able to see the face designs in the rock formations. My friends thought I was "under the influence..."*

Driftwood Porthole ~
This image was a take on an actual piece of driftwood on Westwood Lake near Nanaimo, B.C. It stands about eight feet high and curves into this amazing shape, lending itself to some great interpretation. A magic doorway into an unknown world, perhaps... I took some degree of artistic license, altering it slightly.

Nude ~ *Inspired by love and lost love. A culmination of what was and what could be. A tasteful lighthearted expression of a woman's sexuality and playfulness.*

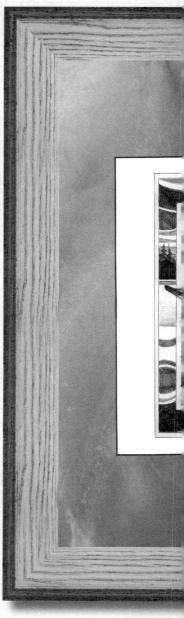

Island Breeze (facing page) ~ *This image was inspired in the days when I would take a hike down to a river or lake and sit on a rock listening to the wind and waves. It was a beautiful time to absorb all the energy and insipration that Mother Nature had to offer. A great way to empty the clutter in the brain and rejuvinate the spirit.*

Moonlit Paddle ~ *For several years friends of mine in the Yukon have been avid kayakers and actually get me out on the water once in a while. It's a great experience and very soothing to the soul.*

Keeper of the Wild ~ *A fantasy image symbolizing "Mother Nature" in an aboriginal-influenced collage.*

Keeper of Broken Hearts ~ *A simple tribute depicting the sadness and heartbreak of love gone wrong.*

Facing Page:
Medicine Fire (left) ~ *This image was a tribute to a proud and noble people and their ways before the white man's influence.*

Warmth (right) ~ *A beautiful maiden wrapped up in a warm blanket while a gentle breeze caresses her long silky hair and tender, soft features of her face and shoulder.*

Campfire Guest ~ *Sitting around a campfire, occasionally you might hear a noise coming from outside your vision. This is a rendering of one scenario of what it could have been. I gave the bear a softer more gentle look and the skull is a reminder that man can be just as dangerous.*

Cabin (top) ~ *A sketch of a simpler life. Ah, to get away from it all and escape the modern headaches of life.*

Raven Moon (bottom) ~ *This print was an accompaniment to the "Cabin". A crackling fire under a full moon - pure therapy.*

The Ocean & Beyond

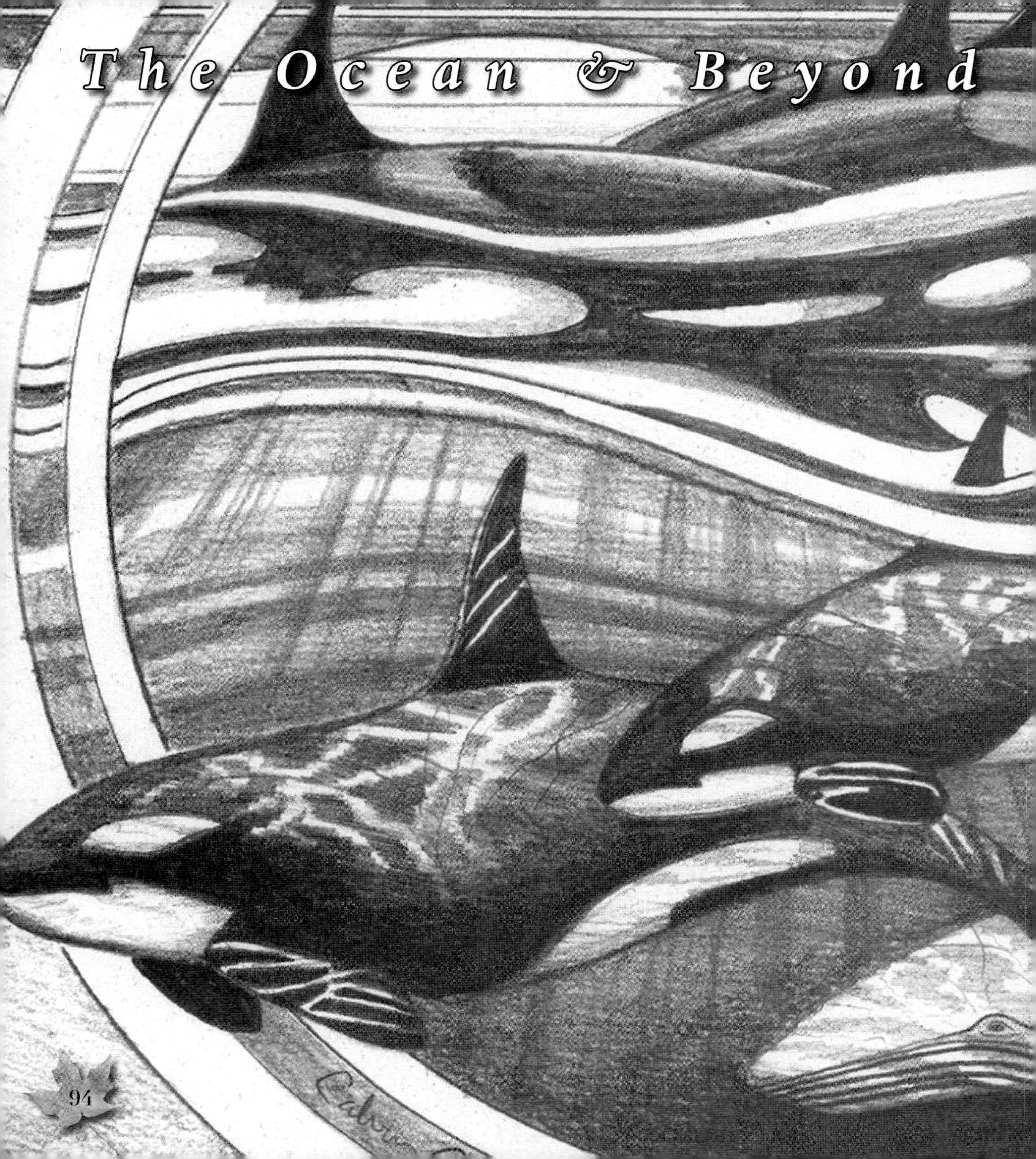

Native Design Orca ~ *My own take on a West Coast aboriginal-influenced image with Haida form and reality mix.*

Dolphins ~ *Many customers were after me for a long time to do a dolphin print. The end product was this image of two dolphins dancing under the surf with the wave-refracted light dancing off their backs. A peaceful, freeing image. The currents sweeping over the dolphin's streamlined bodies.*

Orca And Humpback ~ *Living on Vancouver Island for several years, the influence of Orca scenes seemed to be everywhere. The sea life atmosphere rubbed off a little.*

Panda ~ *This very rare and endangered bear is one of my earlier prints. The Panda to me is a striking figure in nature with its strong black and white contrast.*

Lion ~ *A portrait of the King with the sideburns... Okay, I apologize for my warped sense of humor.*

A Bull African Elephant ~ *A massive presence in the African Plains and a sight to behold, no doubt.*

The Other Stuff

Hummingbird - "Wind On Wing" ~ *A romantic notion of a beautiful native girl with an endearing pet name.*

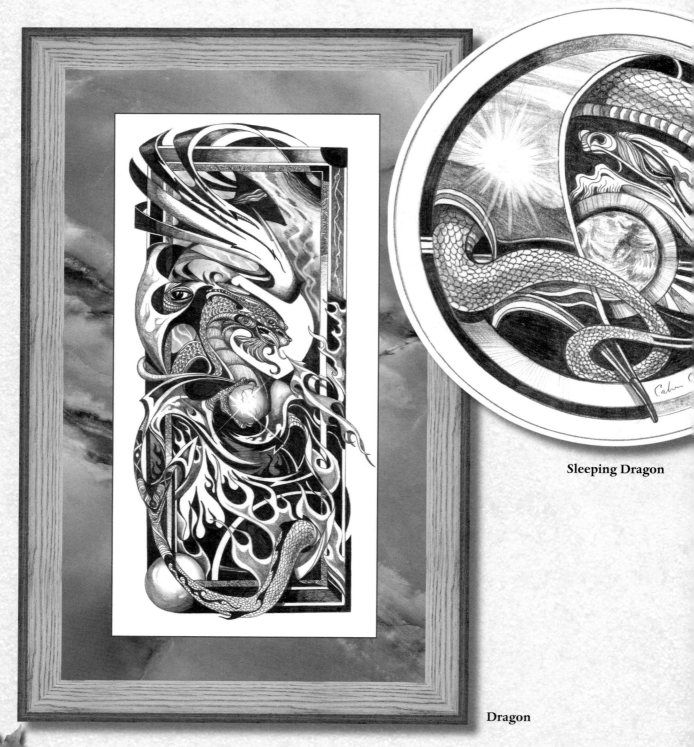

Sleeping Dragon

Dragon

104

Dragon ~ *Before I did mainly nature pictures full time I dabbled in fantasy art. The dragon design was a nostalgic look back into my early days. The fascination with them is still with me today. I tried to give these strong and mystical creatures of folklore a more dynamic and noble look than its usual villified role.*

Love Potion ~ *A fantasy aboriginal-inspired design symbolizing the power a woman has over the hearts of men.*

Phoenix Rising

From the ash of failure, I am reborn stronger, wiser, and more determined.

These four images were inspired by a great love for animals. The proceeds from these images went to help fund SPCA's in White-horse, Dawson Creek, and Grande Prairie.

Joyride Puppies (top left) ~ This picture was inspired by five puppies I found one day abandoned in the Yukon by Lake LaBarge. I found them miles from nowhere, half--starved and only a few months old. I rounded them up and took them to the Humane Society in Whitehorse. I think they only survived as long as they did because of a nearby stream.

Mask - Earth, Wind & Fire
~ This image is my own take on a Haida art design. It is by no means a traditional replication, but I am a great admirer of the art form. It depicts man's influence over nature. Our choices can be a catastrophe, or we could work to protect and preserve the wilderness.

Image Index